*The Zodiac
and Its Signs*

By
Manly P. Hall

Copyright © 2022 Lamp of Trismegistus. All rights reserved. No part of this publication may be reproduced or transmitted in any form or by any means, electronic or mechanical, including photocopying, recording, or by any information storage and retrieval system, without permission in writing from Lamp of Trismegistus. Reviewers may quote brief passages.

ISBN: 978-1-63118-596-0

Esoteric Classics

Other Books in this Series and Related Titles

Aurora of the Philosophers by Paracelsus (978-1-63118-507-6)

Rosicrucian Rules, Secret Signs, Codes and Symbols by various (978-1-63118-488-8)

Ancient Mysteries and Secret Societies by Manly P Hall (978–1–63118–597–7)

Paracelsus, the Four Elements and Their Spirits by M P Hall (978-1-63118-400-0)

The Stone of the Philosophers by A E Waite (978-1-63118-509-0)

Mysterious Wonders of Antiquity by Manly P Hall (978-1-63118-598-4)

The Rosicrucian Chemical Marriage by Christian Rosenkreuz (978-1-63118-458-1)

The Alchemical Catechism of Paracelsus by Paracelsus (978-1-63118-513-7)

Alchemy in the Nineteenth Century by Helena P. Blavatsky (978-1-63118-446-8)

Rosicrucians and Speculative Masonry in the Seventeenth Century (978-1-63118-489-5)

Qabbalistic Teachings and the Tree of Life by M P Hall (978-1-63118-482-6)

The Sepher Yetzirah and the Qabalah by M P Hall (978-1-63118-481-9)

The Devil in Love by Jacques Cazotte (978–1–63118–499–4)

Fortune-Telling with Dice by Astra Cielo (978-1-63118-466-6)

History, Analysis and Secret Tradition of the Tarot by Hall &c (978-1-63118-445-1)

Crystal Vision Through Crystal Gazing by Frater Achad (978-1-63118-455-0)

The Golden Verses of Pythagoras: Five Translations (978-1-63118-479-6)

Arcane Formulas or Mental Alchemy by W W Atkinson (978-1-63118-459-8)

The Machinery of the Mind by Dion Fortune (978-1-63118-451-2)

The A E Waite Reader: A Selection of Occult Essays (978-1-63118-515-1)

The Leadbeater Reader: A Selection of Occult Essays (978-1-63118-483-3)

Audio versions are also available on Audible, Amazon and Apple

Other Books in this Series and Related Titles

Life and Teachings of Hermes Trismegistus by Manly P Hall (978–1–63118–595–3)

The Secrets of Doctor Taverner by Dion Fortune (978–1–63118–594–6)

Vegetarianism, Theosophy & Occultism by Leadbeater &c (978–1–63118–593–9)

Applied Theosophy by Henry S Olcott (978–1–63118–592–2)

Higher Consciousness by C W Leadbeater (978–1–63118–591–5)

Theories About Reincarnation and Spirits by H P Blavatsky (978–1–63118–590–8)

The Use and Power of Thought by C W Leadbeater (978–1–63118–589–2)

Commentary on the Pymander by G R S Mead (978–1–63118–588–5)

Hypnotism and Mesmerism by Annie Besant (978–1–63118–587–8)

Spirits of Various Kinds by Helena P Blavatsky (978–1–63118–586–1)

The Hidden Language of Symbolism by Annie Besant (978–1–63118–585–4)

Eastern Magic & Western Spiritualism by Henry S Olcott (978–1–63118–584–7)

Spiritual Progress and Practical Occultism by H P Blavatsky (978–1–63118–583–0)

Memory and Consciousness by Besant & Blavatsky (978–1–63118–582–3)

The Origin of Evil by Helena P Blavatsky (978–1–63118–581–6)

The Camp of Philosophy: Studies in Alchemy by Bloomfield (978–1–63118–580–9)

The Testaments of the Twelve Patriarchs (978–1–63118–579–3)

Occult or Exact Science? by Helena P Blavatsky (978–1–63118–578–6)

Occultism, Semi-Occultism & Pseudo Occultism by A Besant (978–1–63118–577–9)

The Fourth-Gospel and Synoptical Problem by G R S Mead (978–1–63118–576–2)

On the Bhagavad-Gita by T Subba Row &c (978–1–63118–575–5)

Audio versions are also available on Audible, Amazon and Apple

Table of Contents

Introduction...7

The Zodiac and Its Signs...9

How the Elements are in the Heavens, in Stars, in Devils, in Angels, and Lastly in God Himself
by Eliphas Levi...31

INTRODUCTION

The word "esoteric" can be difficult to define. Esotericism in general can be seen less as a system of beliefs and more as a category, which encompasses numerous, different systems of beliefs. It's a bit of juxtaposition, since the word "esoteric" indicates something that few people know about, while the term itself broadly covers numerous philosophies, practices, areas of study and belief systems.

In a greater sense, Esotericism acts as a storehouse for secret knowledge, which is often considered ancient (by *tradition, if not by fact),* passed down from generation to generation, in private. At various times in history, simply possessing the knowledge of some of these subjects, was considered illegal and a jailable offence, if discovered. This usually included such general topics as Alchemy, Pharmacology, Qabalah, Hermeticism, Occultism, Ceremonial Magic, Astrology, Divination, Rosicrucianism and so on. Collectively, these areas of study were often referred to as the esoteric sciences.

Sometimes, the outer garment of a subject isn't esoteric, while what is hidden beneath it, is. As an example, Freemasonry isn't necessarily esoteric by nature (at *least not anymore),* but certain signs, passwords and handshakes given to the candidate during their initiation, are in fact, esoteric, in the sense that they are hidden from the general public.

Today, in the twenty-first century, such topics are readily available at bookstores across the country, and numerous mainsteam publishers offer beginners guides and coffee-table volumes on many of these subjects, intended for mass appeal. Books like *"The Secret"* have turned previously arcane topics into household knowledge. All that being the case, however, it isn't to say that there still aren't buried secrets to uncover, ancient wisdom being ignored and forgotten mysteries to be explored. In fact, it is often that we are only able to further our own studies by standing on the shoulders of these disappearing giants.

Lamp of Trismegistus is doing its part to help preserve humanity's esoteric history by making some of these classics available to those students who are seeking to unearth the knowledge of these ancient colossi.

So, be sure to check other titles from our *Esoteric Classics* series, as well as our *Occult Fiction, Theosophical Classics, Foundations of Freemasonry Series, Supernatural Fiction, Paranormal Research Series, Studies in Buddhism* and our *Christian Apocrypha Series*. You can also download the audio versions of most of these titles from Amazon, Apple or Audible, for learning on the go.

THE ZODIAC AND ITS SIGNS

IT is difficult for this age to estimate correctly the profound effect produced upon the religions, philosophies, and sciences of antiquity by the study of the planets, luminaries, and constellations. Not without adequate reason were the Magi of Persia called the Star Gazers. The Egyptians were honored with a special appellation because of their proficiency in computing the power and motion of the heavenly bodies and their effect upon the destinies of nations and individuals. Ruins of primitive astronomical observatories have been discovered in all parts of the world, although in many cases modern archæologists are unaware of the true purpose for which these structures were erected. While the telescope was unknown to ancient astronomers, they made many remarkable calculations with instruments cut from blocks of granite or pounded from sheets of brass and cop per. In India such instruments are still in use, and they posses a high degree of accuracy. In Jaipur, Rajputana, India, an observatory consisting largely of immense stone sundials is still in operation. The famous Chinese observatory on the wall of Peking consists of immense bronze instruments, including a telescope in the form of a hollow tube without lenses.

The pagans looked upon the stars as living things, capable of influencing the destinies of individuals, nations, and races. That the early Jewish patriarchs believed that the celestial bodies participated in the affairs of men is evident to any student of Biblical literature, as, for example, in the Book of Judges: "They fought from heaven, even the stars in their courses fought against Sisera." The Chaldeans, Phœnicians, Egyptians, Persians, Hindus, and Chinese all had zodiacs that were much alike in general character, and different authorities have credited each of these nations with being the cradle of astrology and astronomy. The Central and North American

Indians also had an understanding of the zodiac, but the patterns and numbers of the signs differed in many details from those of the Eastern Hemisphere.

The word *zodiac* is derived from the Greek ζωδιακός (*zodiakos*), which means "a circle of animals," or, as some believe, "little animals." It is the name given by the old pagan astronomers to a band of fixed stars about sixteen degrees wide, apparently encircling the earth. Robert Hewitt Brown, 32°, states that the Greek word zodiakos comes from *zo-on*, meaning "an animal." He adds: "This latter word is compounded directly from the primitive Egyptian radicals, *zo*, life, and *on*, a being."

The Greeks, and later other peoples influenced by their culture, divided the band of the zodiac into twelve sections, each being sixteen degrees in width and thirty degrees in length. These divisions were called the Houses of the Zodiac. The sun during its annual pilgrimage passed through each of these in turn, Imaginary creatures were traced in the Star groups bounded by these rectangles; and because most of them were animal--or part animal--in form, they later became known as the Constellations, or Signs, of the Zodiac.

There is a popular theory concerning the origin of the zodiacal creatures to the effect that they were products of the imagination of shepherds, who, watching their flocks at night, occupied their minds by tracing the forms of animals and birds in the heavens. This theory is untenable, unless the "shepherds" be regarded as the shepherd priests of antiquity. It is unlikely that the zodiacal signs were derived from the star groups which they now represent. It is far more probable that the creatures assigned to the twelve houses are symbolic of the qualities and intensity of the sun's power while it occupies different parts of the zodiacal belt.

On this subject Richard Payne Knight writes: "The emblematical meaning, which certain animals were employed to signify, was only some particular property generalized; and, therefore, might easily be invented or discovered by the natural operation of the mind: but the collections of stars, named after certain animals, have no resemblance whatever to those animals; which are therefore merely signs of convention adopted to distinguish certain portions of the heavens, which were probably consecrated to those particular personified attributes, which they respectively represented." (*The Symbolical Language of Ancient Art and Mythology.*)

Some authorities are of the opinion that the zodiac was originally divided into ten (instead of twelve) houses, or "solar mansions." In early times there were two separate standards--one solar and the other lunar--used for the measurement of the months, years, and seasons. The solar year was composed of ten months of thirty-six days each, and five days sacred to the gods. The lunar year consisted of thirteen months of twenty-eight days each, with one day left over. The solar zodiac at that time consisted often houses of thirty-six degrees each.

The first six signs of the zodiac of twelve signs were regarded as benevolent, because the sun occupied them while traversing the Northern Hemisphere. The 6,000 years during which, according to the Persians, Ahura-Mazda ruled His universe in harmony and peace, were symbolic of these six signs. The second six were considered malevolent, because while the sun was traveling the Southern Hemisphere it was winter with the Greeks, Egyptians, and Persians. Therefore these six months symbolic of the 6,000 years of misery and suffering caused by the evil genius of the Persians, Ahriman, who sought to overthrow the power of Ahura-Mazda.

Those who hold the opinion that before its revision by the Greeks the zodiac consisted of only ten signs adduce evidence to show that Libra (the Scales) was inserted into the zodiac by dividing the constellation of Virgo Scorpio (at that time one sign) into two parts, thus establishing "the balance" at the point of equilibrium between the ascending northern and the descending southern signs. (See *The Rosicrucians, Their Rites and Mysteries*, by Hargrave Jennings.) On this subject Isaac Myer states: "We think that the Zodiacal constellations were first ten and represented an immense androgenic

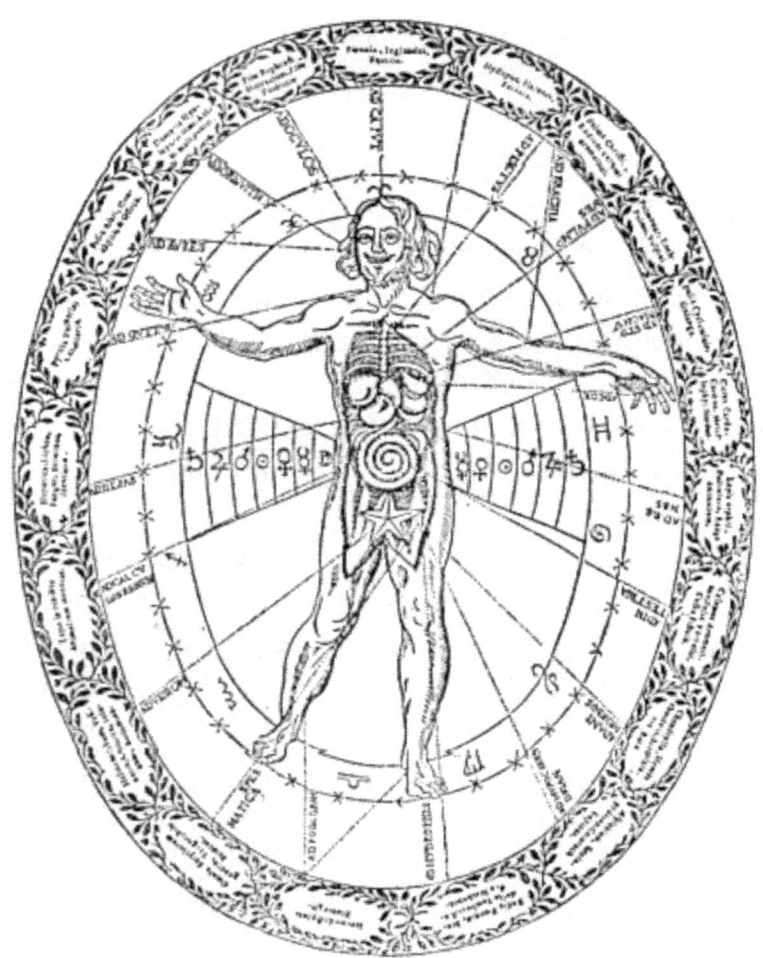

CHART SHOWING THE RELATIONSHIP BETWEEN THE HUMAN BODY AND THE EXTERIOR UNIVERSE[1]

---

[1] Image from Kircher's *Œdipus Ægyptiacus*.

The ornamental border contains groups of names of animal, mineral, and vegetable substances, Their relationship to corresponding parts of the human body is shown by the dotted lines. The words in capital letters on the dotted lines indicate to what corporeal member, organ, or disease, the herb or other substance is related. The favorable positions in

man or deity; subsequently this was changed, resulting in Scorpio and Virgo and making eleven; after this from Scorpio, Libra, the Balance, was taken, making the present twelve." (*The Qabbalah.*)

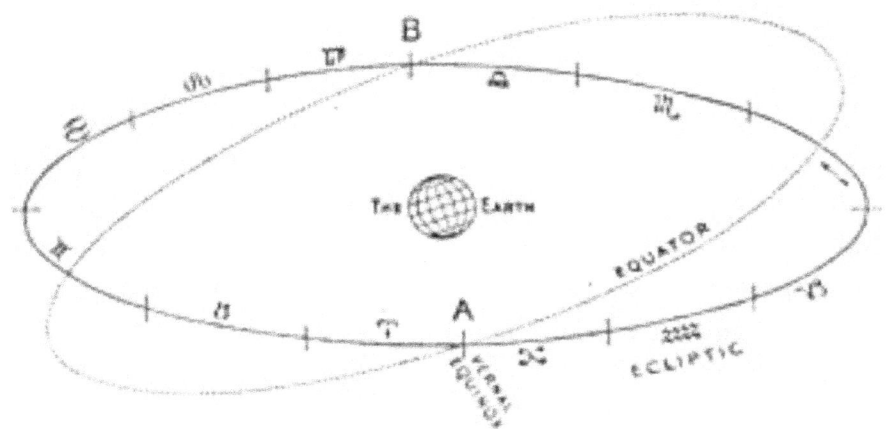

THE EQUINOXES AND SOLSTICES[2]

Each year the sun passes entirely around the zodiac and returns to the point from which it started--the vernal equinox--and each year it falls just a little short of making the complete circle of the heavens in the allotted period of time. As a result, it crosses the equator just a little behind the spot in the zodiacal sign where it crossed the previous year. Each sign of the zodiac consists of thirty degrees, and as the sun loses about one degree every seventy two years, it regresses through one entire constellation (or sign) in approximately 2,160 years, and through the entire zodiac in about 25,920 years.

---

relation to the time of year are shown by the signs of the zodiac, each house of which is divided by crosses into its three decans. This influence is further emphasized by the series of planetary signs placed on either side of the figure.

[2] The plane of the zodiac intersects the celestial equator at an angle of approximately 23° 28'. The two points of intersection (A and B) are called the equinoxes.

(Authorities disagree concerning these figures.) This retrograde motion is called the *precession of the equinoxes*. This means that in the course of about 25,920 years, which constitute one Great Solar or Platonic Year, each one of the twelve constellations occupies a position at the vernal equinox for nearly 2,160 years, then gives place to the *previous* sign.

Among the ancients the sun was always symbolized by the figure and nature of the constellation through which it passed at the vernal equinox. For nearly the past 2,000 years the sun has crossed the equator at the vernal equinox in the constellation of Pisces (the Two Fishes). For the 2,160 years before that it crossed through the constellation of Aries (the Ram). Prior to that the vernal equinox was in the sign of Taurus (the Bull). It is probable that the form of the bull and the bull's proclivities were assigned to this constellation because the bull was used by the ancients to plow the fields, and the season set aside for plowing and furrowing corresponded to the time at which the sun reached the segment of the heavens named Taurus.

Albert Pike describes the reverence which the Persians felt for this sign and the method of astrological symbolism in vogue among them, thus: "In Zoroaster's cave of initiation, the Sun and Planets were represented, overhead, in gems and gold, as was also the Zodiac. The Sun appeared, emerging from the back of Taurus. " In the constellation of the Bull are also to be found the "Seven Sisters"--the sacred Pleiades--famous to Freemasonry as the Seven Stars at the upper end of the Sacred Ladder.

In ancient Egypt it was during this period--when the vernal equinox was in the sign of Taurus--that the Bull, Apis, was sacred to the Sun God, who was worshiped through the animal equivalent of the celestial sign which he had impregnated with his presence at the time of its crossing into the Northern Hemisphere. This is the meaning of an ancient saying that the celestial Bull "broke the egg of the year with his horns."

Sampson Arnold Mackey, in his *Mythological Astronomy of the Ancients Demonstrated*, makes note of two very interesting points concerning the bull in Egyptian symbolism. Mr. Mackey is of the opinion that the motion of the earth that we know as the alternation of the poles has resulted in a great change of relative position of the equator and the zodiacal band. He believes that originally the band of the zodiac was at right angles to the equator, with the sign of Cancer opposite the north pole and the sign of Capricorn opposite the south pole. It is possible that the Orphic symbol of the serpent twisted around the egg attempts to show the motion of the sun in relation to the earth under such conditions. Mr. Mackey advances the *Labyrinth of Crete*, the name *Abraxas*, and the magic formula, *abracadabra*, among other things, to substantiate his theory. Concerning *abracadabra* he states:

"But the slow progressive disappearance of the Bull is most happily commemorated in the vanishing series of letters so emphatically expressive of the great astronomical fact. For ABRACADABRA is The Bull, the only Bull. The ancient sentence split into its component parts stands thus: Ab'r-achad-ab'ra, *i. e.*, Ab'r, the Bull; achad, the only, &c.--Achad is one of the names of the Sun, given him in consequence of his Shining ALONE,--he is the ONLY Star to be seen when he is seen--the remaining ab'ra, makes the whole to be, The Bull, the only Bull; while the repetition of the name omitting a letter, till all is gone, is the most simple, yet the most satisfactory method that could have been devised to preserve the memory of the fact; and the name of Sorapis, or Serapis, given to the Bull at the above ceremony puts it beyond all doubt. * * * This word (Abracadabra) disappears in eleven decreasing stages; as in the figure. And what is very remarkable, a body with three heads is folded up by a Serpent with eleven Coils, and placed by Sorapis: and the eleven Volves of the Serpent form a triangle similar to that formed by the ELEVEN diminishing lines of the abracadabra."

Nearly every religion of the world shows traces of astrological influence. The Old Testament of the Jews, its writings overshadowed by Egyptian culture, is a mass of astrological and astronomical allegories. Nearly all the mythology of Greece and Rome may be traced in star groups. Some writers are of the opinion that the original twenty-two letters of the Hebrew alphabet were derived from groups of stars, and that the starry handwriting on the wall of the heavens referred to words spelt out, with fixed stars for consonants, and the planets, or luminaries, for vowels. These, coming into ever-different combinations, spelt words which, when properly read, foretold future events.

As the zodiacal band marks the pathway of the sun through the constellations, it results in the phenomena of the seasons. The ancient systems of measuring the year were based upon the equinoxes and the solstices. The year always began with the vernal equinox, celebrated March 21 with rejoicing to mark the moment when the sun crossed the equator northward up the zodiacal arc. The summer solstice was celebrated when the sun reached its most northerly position, and the day appointed was June 21. After that time the sun began to descend toward the equator, which it recrossed southbound at the autumnal equinox, September 21. The sun reached its most southerly position at the winter solstice, December 21.

Four of the signs of the zodiac have been permanently dedicated to the equinoxes and the solstices; and, while the signs no longer correspond with the ancient constellations to which they were assigned, and from which they secured their names, they are accepted by modern astronomers as a basis of calculation. The vernal equinox is therefore said to occur in the constellation of Aries (the Ram). It is fitting that of all beasts a Ram should be placed at the head of the heavenly flock forming the zodiacal band. Centuries before the Christian Era, the pagans revered this constellation. Godfrey Higgins states: "This constellation was called the 'Lamb of God.' He was also called the 'Savior,' and was said to save mankind from their sins. He was always honored with the appellation of 'Dominus' or 'Lord.' He was called the 'Lamb of God which taketh away the sins of the world.' The devotees addressing him in their litany, constantly repeated the words, 'O Lamb of God, that taketh away the sin of the world, have mercy upon us. Grant us Thy peace.'" Therefore, the *Lamb of God* is a title given to the sun, who is said to be reborn every year in the Northern Hemisphere in the sign of the Ram, although, due to the existing discrepancy between the signs of the zodiac and the actual star groups, it actually rises in the sign of Pisces.

The summer solstice is regarded as occurring in Cancer (the Crab), which the Egyptians called the *scarab*--a beetle of the family Lamellicornes, the head of the insect kingdom, and sacred to the Egyptians as the symbol of Eternal Life. It is evident that the constellation of the Crab is represented by this peculiar creature because the sun, after passing through this house, proceeds to walk backwards, or descend the zodiacal arc. Cancer is the symbol of generation, for it is the house of the Moon, the great Mother of all things and the patroness of the life forces of Nature. Diana, the moon goddess of the Greeks, is called the Mother of the World. Concerning the worship of the feminine or maternal principle, Richard Payne Knight writes:

"By attracting or heaving the waters of the ocean, she naturally appeared to be the sovereign of humidity; and by seeming to operate so powerfully upon the constitutions of women, she equally appeared to be the patroness and regulatress of nutrition and passive generation: whence she is said to have received her nymphs, or subordinate personifications, from the ocean; and is often represented by the symbol of the sea crab, an animal that has the property of spontaneously detaching from its own body any limb that has been hurt or mutilated, and reproducing another in its place." (*The Symbolical Language of Ancient Art and Mythology.*) This water sign, being symbolic of the maternal principle of Nature, and recognized by the pagans as the origin of all life, was a natural and consistent domicile of the moon.

The autumnal equinox apparently occurs in the constellation of Libra (the Balances). The scales tipped and the solar globe began its pilgrimage toward the house of winter. The constellation of the Scales was placed in the zodiac to symbolize the power of choice, by means of which man may weigh one problem against another. Millions of years ago, when the human race was in the making, man was like the angels, who knew neither good nor evil. He *fell* into the state of the knowledge of good and evil when the gods gave him the seed for the mental nature. From man's mental reactions to his environments he distills the product of experience, which then aids him to regain his lost position plus an individualized intelligence. Paracelsus said: "The body comes from the elements, the soul from the stars, and the spirit from God. All that the intellect can conceive of comes from the stars [the spirits of the stars, rather than the material constellations]."

The constellation of Capricorn, in which the winter solstice theoretically takes place, was called *The House of Death*, for in winter all life in the Northern Hemisphere is at its lowest ebb. Capricorn is a composite creature, with the head and upper body of a goat and the tail of a fish. In this constellation the sun is least powerful in the

Northern Hemisphere, and after passing through this constellation it immediately begins to increase. Hence the Greeks said that Jupiter

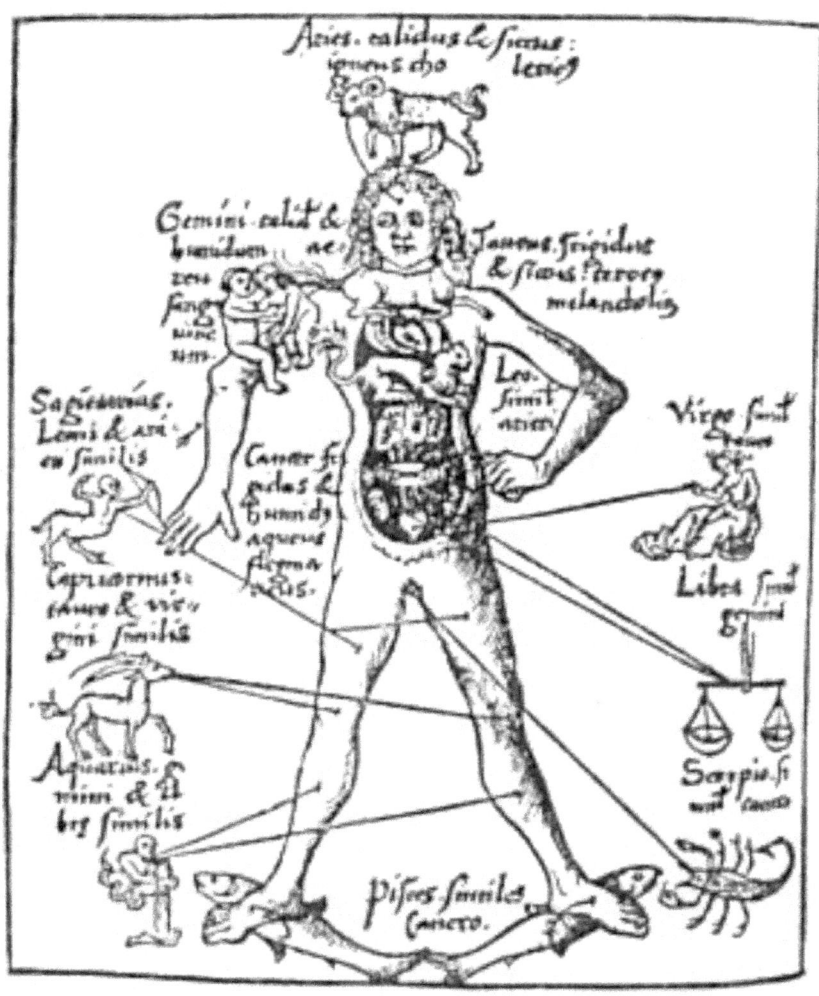

THE MICROCOSM[3]

---

[3] Image from Schotus' *Margarita Philosophica*.

The pagans believed that the zodiac formed the body of the Grand Man of the Universe. This body, which they called the Macrocosm (the Great World), was divided into twelve major parts, one of which was under the control of the celestial powers reposing in each of the zodiacal constellations. Believing that the entire universal system was epitomized in man's body, which they called the Microcosm (the Little World), they evolved that now familiar (a name of the Sun God) was suckled by a goat. A new and different sidelight on zodiacal symbolism is supplied by John Cole, in *A Treatise on the Circular Zodiac of Tentyra, in Egypt*: "The symbol therefore of the Goat rising from the body of a fish [Capricorn], represents with the greatest propriety the mountainous buildings of Babylon rising out of its low and marshy situation; the two horns of the Goat being emblematical of the two towns, Nineveh and Babylon, the former built on the Tigris, the latter on the Euphrates; but both subjected to one sovereignty."

The period of 2,160 years required for the regression of the sun through one of the zodiacal constellations is often termed an age. According to this system, the age secured its name from the sign through which the sun passes year after year as it crosses the equator at the vernal equinox. From this arrangement are derived the terms *The Taurian Age*, *The Aryan Age*, *The Piscean Age*, and *The Aquarian Age*. During these periods, or ages, religious worship takes the form of the appropriate celestial sign--that which the sun is said to assume as a personality in the same manner that a spirit assumes a body. These twelve signs are the jewels of his breastplate and his light shines forth from them, one after the other.

From a consideration of this system, it is readily understood why certain religious symbols were adopted during different ages of the earth's history; for during the 2,160 years the sun was in the constellation of Taurus, it is said that the Solar Deity assumed the body of Apis, and the Bull became sacred to Osiris. (For details concerning the astrological ages as related to Biblical symbolism, see *The Message of the Stars* by Max and Augusta Foss Heindel.)

---

figure of "the cut-up man in the almanac" by allotting a sign of the zodiac to each of twelve major parts of the human body.

During the Aryan Age the Lamb was held sacred and the priests were called *shepherds*. Sheep and goats were sacrificed upon the altars, and a scapegoat was appointed to bear the sins of Israel.

During the Age of Pisces, the Fish was the symbol of divinity and the Sun God fed the multitude with two small fishes. The frontispiece of Inman's *Ancient Faiths* shows the goddess Isis with a fish on her head; and the Indian Savior God, Christna, in one of his incarnations was cast from the mouth of a fish.

Not only is Jesus often referred to as the *Fisher of Men*, but as John P. Lundy writes: "The word Fish is an abbreviation of this whole title, Jesus Christ, Son of God, Savior, and Cross; or as St. Augustine expresses it, 'If you join together the initial letters of the five Greek words, Ἰησοῦς Χριστος Θεου Υιὸσ Σωτήρ, which mean Jesus Christ, Son of God, Savior, they will make ΙΧΘΥΣ, Fish, in which word Christ is mystically understood, because He was able to live in the abyss of this mortality as in the depth of waters, that is, without sin.'" (*Monumental Christianity*.) Many Christians observe Friday, which is sacred to the Virgin (Venus), upon which day they shall eat fish and not meat. The sign of the fish was one of the earliest symbols of Christianity; and when drawn upon the sand, it informed one Christian that another of the same faith was near.

Aquarius is called the *Sign of the Water Bearer*, or the man with a jug of water on his shoulder mentioned in the New Testament. This is sometimes shown as an angelic figure, supposedly androgynous, either pouring water from an urn or carrying the vessel upon its shoulder. Among Oriental peoples, a water vessel alone is often used. Edward Upham, in his *History and Doctrine of Budhism*, describes Aquarius as being "in the shape of a pot and of a color between blue and yellow; this Sign is the single house of Saturn."

When Herschel discovered the planet Uranus (sometimes called by the name of its discoverer), the second half of the sign of Aquarius was allotted to this added member of the planetary family. The water pouring from the urn of Aquarius under the name of "the waters of eternal life" appears many times in symbolism. So it is with all the signs. Thus the sun in its path controls whatever form of worship man offers to the Supreme Deity.

There are two distinct systems of astrological philosophy. One of them, the Ptolemaic, is geocentric: the earth is considered the center of the solar system, around which the sun, moon, and planets revolve. Astronomically, the geocentric system is incorrect; but for thousands of years it has proved its accuracy when applied to the material nature of earthly things. A careful consideration of the writings of the great occultists and a study of their diagrams reveal the fact that many of them were acquainted with another method of arranging the heavenly bodies.

The other system of astrological philosophy is called the heliocentric. This posits the sun in the center of the solar system, where it naturally belongs, with the planets and their moons revolving about it. The great difficulty, however, with the heliocentric system is that, being comparatively new, there has not been sufficient time to experiment successfully and catalogue the effects of its various aspects and relationships. Geocentric astrology, as its name implies, is confined to the earthy side of nature, while heliocentric astrology may be used to analyze the higher intellectual and spiritual faculties of man.

The important point to be remembered is that when the sun was said to be in a certain sign of the zodiac, the ancients really meant that the sun occupied the opposite sign and cast its long ray into the house in which they enthroned it. Therefore, when it is said that the sun is in Taurus, it means (astronomically) that the sun is in the sign opposite to Taurus, which is Scorpio. This resulted in two distinct schools of philosophy: one geocentric and exoteric, the other heliocentric and esoteric. While the ignorant multitudes worshiped the house of the sun's reflection, which in the case described would be the Bull, the wise revered the house of the sun's actual dwelling, which would be the Scorpion, or the Serpent, the symbol of the concealed spiritual mystery. This sign has three different symbols. The most common is that of a Scorpion, who was called by the ancients the *backbiter*, being the symbol of deceit and perversion; the second (and less common) form of the sign is a Serpent, often used by the ancients to symbolize wisdom.

Probably the rarest form of Scorpio is that of an Eagle. The arrangement of the stars of the constellation bears as much resemblance to a flying bird as to a scorpion. Scorpio, being the sign of occult initiation, the flying eagle--the king of birds--represents the highest and most spiritual type of Scorpio, in which it transcends the venomous insect of the earth. As Scorpio and Taurus are opposite each other in the zodiac, their symbolism is often closely intermingled. The Hon. E. M. Plunket, in *Ancient Calendars and Constellations*, says: "The Scorpion (the constellation Scorpio of the Zodiac opposed to Taurus) joins with Mithras in his attack upon the Bull, and always the genii of the spring and autumn equinoxes are present in joyous and mournful attitudes."

The Egyptians, the Assyrians, and the Babylonians, who knew the sun as a Bull, called the zodiac a series of furrows, through which the great celestial Ox dragged the plow of the sun. Hence the populace offered up sacrifice and led through the streets magnificent steers, bedecked with flowers and surrounded with priests, dancing girls of the temple, and musicians. The philosophic elect did not participate in these idolatrous ceremonials, but advocated them as most suitable for the types of mind composing the mass of the population. These few possessed a far deeper understanding, as the Serpent of Scorpio upon their foreheads-- the *Uræus*--bore witness.

THE CIRCULAR ZODIAC OF TENTYRA[4]

---

[4] Image from Cole's *Treatise--the Circular Zodiac of Tentyra, in Egypt*.

The oldest circular zodiac known is the one found at Tentyra, in Egypt, and now in the possession of the French government. Mr. John Cole describes this remarkable zodiac as follows: "The diameter of the medallion in which the constellations are sculptured, is four feet nine inches, French measure. It is surrounded by another circle of much larger circumference, containing hieroglyphic characters; this second circle is enclosed in a square, whose sides are seven feet nine inches long. * * * The asterisms, constituting the Zodiacal constellations mixed with others, are represented in a spiral. The extremities of this spiral, after one revolution, are Leo and Cancer. Leo is no doubt at the head. It appears to be trampling on a serpent, and its tail to be held by a woman. Immediately after the Lion comes the Virgin holding an ear of corn, Further on, we perceive two scales of a balance, above

The sun is often symbolized with its rays in the form of a shaggy mane. Concerning the Masonic significance of Leo, Robert Hewitt Brown, 32°, has written: "On the 21st of June, when the sun arrives at the summer solstice, the constellation Leo--being but 30° in advance of the sun--appears to be leading the way, and to aid by his powerful paw in lifting the sun up to the summit of the zodiacal arch. * * * This visible connection between the constellation Leo and the return of the sun to his place of power and glory, at the summit of the Royal Arch of heaven, was the principal reason why that constellation was held in such high esteem and reverence by the ancients. The astrologers distinguished Leo as the 'sole house of the sun,' and taught that the world was created when the sun was in that sign. 'The lion was adored in the East and the West by the Egyptians and the Mexicans. The chief Druid of Britain was styled a lion.'" (*Stellar Theology and Masonic Astronomy*.) When the Aquarian Age is thoroughly established, the sun will be in Leo, as will be noted from the explanation previously given in this chapter regarding the distinction between geocentric and heliocentric astrology. Then, indeed, will the secret religions of the world include once more the raising to initiation by the Grip of the Lion's Paw. (Lazarus will come forth.)

The antiquity of the zodiac is much in dispute. To contend that it originated but a mere few thousand years before the Christian Era is a colossal mistake on the part of those who have sought to compile data, concerning its origin. The zodiac necessarily must be ancient enough to go backward to that period when its signs and

---

which, in a medal lion, is the figure of Harpocrates. Then follows the Scorpion and Sagittarius, to whom the Egyptians gave wings, and two faces. After Sagittarius are successively placed, Capricornus, Aquarius, Pisces, the Ram, the Bull, and the Twins. This Zodiacal procession is, as we have already observed, terminated by Cancer, the Crab."

symbols coincided exactly with the positions of the constellations whose various creatures in their natural functions exemplified the outstanding features of the sun's activity during each of the twelve months. One author, after many years of deep study on the subject, believed man's concept of the zodiac to be at least five million years old. In all probability it is one of the many things for which the modern world is indebted to the Atlantean or the Lemurian civilizations. About ten thousand years before the Christian Era there was a period of many ages when knowledge of every kind was suppressed, tablets destroyed, monuments torn down, and every vestige of available material concerning previous civilizations completely obliterated. Only a few copper knives, some arrowheads, and crude carvings on the walls of caves bear mute witness of those civilizations which preceded this age of destruction. Here and there a few gigantic structures have remained which, like the strange monoliths on Easter Island, are evidence of lost arts and sciences and lost races. The human race is exceedingly old. Modern science counts its age in tens of thousands of years; occultism, in tens of millions. There is an old saying that "Mother Earth has shaken many civilizations from her back," and it is not beyond reason that the principles of astrology and astronomy were evolved millions of years before the first white man appeared.

The occultists of the ancient world had a most remarkable understanding of the principle of evolution. They recognized all life as being in various stages of *becoming*. They believed that grains of sand were in the process of *becoming* human in consciousness but not necessarily in form; that human creatures were in the process of *becoming* planets; that planets were in the process of *becoming* solar systems; and that solar systems were in the process of *becoming* cosmic chains; and so on *ad infinitum*. One of the stages between the solar system and the cosmic chain was called the *zodiac*; therefore they taught that at a certain time a solar system breaks up into a zodiac. The house of the zodiac become the thrones for twelve Celestial Hierarchies, or as certain of the ancients state, ten Divine Orders. Pythagoras taught that 10, or the unit of the decimal system, was the most perfect of all numbers, and he symbolized the number ten by the *lesser tetractys*, an arrangement of ten dots in the form of an upright triangle.

The early star gazers, after dividing the zodiac into its houses, appointed the three brightest scars in each constellation to be the joint rulers of that house. Then they divided the house into three sections of ten degrees each, which they called decans. These, in turn, were divided in half, resulting in the breaking up of the zodiac into seventy-two duodecans of five degrees each. Over each of these duodecans the Hebrews placed a celestial intelligence, or angel, and from this system, has resulted the Qabbalistic arrangement of the seventy-two sacred names, which correspond to the seventy-two flowers, knops, and almonds upon the seven-branched Candlestick of the Tabernacle, and the seventy-two men who were chosen from the Twelve Tribes to represent Israel.

The only two signs not already mentioned are Gemini and Sagittarius. The constellation of Gemini is generally represented as two small children, who, according to the ancients, were born out of eggs, possibly the ones that the Bull broke with his horns. The stories concerning Castor and Pollux, and Romulus and Remus, may be the result of amplifying the myths of these celestial Twins. The symbols of Gemini have passed through many modifications. The one used by the Arabians was the peacock. Two of the important stars in the constellation of Gemini still bear the names of Castor and Pollux. The sign of Gemini is supposed to have been the patron of phallic worship, and the two obelisks, or pillars, in front of temples and churches convey the same symbolism as the Twins.

The sign of Sagittarius consists of what the ancient Greeks called a centaur--a composite creature, the lower half of whose body was in the form of a horse, while the upper half was human. The centaur is generally shown with a bow and arrow in his hands, aiming a shaft far off into the stars. Hence Sagittarius stands for two distinct principles: first, it represents the spiritual evolution of man, for the human form is rising from the body of the beast; secondly, it is the symbol of aspiration and ambition, for as the centaur aims his arrow at the stars, so every human creature aims at a higher mark than he can reach.

Albert Churchward, in *The Signs and Symbols of Primordial Man*, sums up the influence of the zodiac upon religious symbolism in the following words: "The division here [is] in twelve parts, the twelve signs of the Zodiac, twelve tribes of Israel, twelve gates of heaven mentioned in Revelation, and twelve entrances or portals to be passed through in the Great Pyramid, before finally reaching the highest degree, and twelve Apostles in the Christian doctrines, and the twelve original and perfect points in Masonry."

The ancients believed that the theory of man's being made in the image of God was to be understood literally. They maintained that the universe was a great organism not unlike the human body, and that every phase and function of the Universal Body had a correspondence in man. The most precious Key to Wisdom that the priests communicated to the new initiates was what they termed *the law of analogy*. Therefore, to the ancients, the study of the stars was a sacred science, for they saw in the movements of the celestial bodies the ever-present activity of the Infinite Father.

The Pythagoreans were often undeservedly criticized for promulgating the so-called doctrine of metempsychosis, or the transmigration of souls. This concept as circulated among the uninitiated was merely a blind, however, to conceal a sacred truth.

Greek mystics believed that the spiritual nature of man descended into material existence from the Milky Way--the seed ground of souls--through one of the twelve gates of the great zodiacal band. The spiritual nature was therefore said to incarnate in the form of the symbolic creature created by Magian star gazers to represent the

HIEROGLYPHIC PLAN, By HERMES, OF THE ANCIENT ZODIAC[5]

---

[5] Image from Kircher's *Œdipus Ægyptiacus*.

The inner circle contains the hieroglyph of Hemphta, the triform and pantamorphic deity. In the six concentric bands surrounding the inner circle are (from within outward): (1) the numbers of the zodiacal houses in figures and also in words; (2) the modern names of the houses.(3) the Greek or the Egyptian names of the Egyptian deities assigned to the houses; (4) the complete figures of these deities; (5) the ancient or the modem zodiacal signs, sometimes both; (6) the number of decans or subdivisions of the houses.

various zodiacal constellations. If the spirit incarnated through the sign of Aries, it was said to be born in the body of a ram; if in Taurus, in the body of the celestial bull. All human beings were thus symbolized by twelve mysterious creatures through the natures of which they were able to incarnate into the material world. The theory of transmigration was not applicable to the visible material body of man, but rather to the invisible immaterial spirit wandering along the pathway of the stars and sequentially assuming in the course of evolution the forms of the sacred zodiacal animals.

In the Third Book of the *Mathesis* of Julius Firmicus Maternus appears the following extract concerning the positions of the heavenly bodies at the time of the establishment of the inferior universe: "According to Æsculapius, therefore, and Anubius, to whom especially the divinity Mercury committed the secrets of the astrological science, the geniture of the world is as follows: They constituted the Sun in the 15th part of Leo, the Moon in the 15th part of Cancer, Saturn in the 15th part of Capricorn, Jupiter in the 15th part of Sagittary, Mars in the 15th part of Scorpio, Venus in the 15th part of Libra, Mercury in the 15th part of Virgo, and the Horoscope in the 15th part of Cancer. Conformably to this geniture, therefore, to these conditions of the stars, and the testimonies which they adduce in confirmation of this geniture, they are of opinion that the destinies of men, also, are disposed in accordance with the above arrangement, as maybe learnt from that book of Æsculapius which is called Μυριογενεσις, (i.e. Ten Thousand, or an innumerable multitude of Genitures) in order that nothing in the several genitures of men may be found to be discordant with the above-mentioned geniture of the world." The seven ages of man are under the control of the planets in the following order: infancy, the moon; childhood, Mercury; adolescence, Venus; maturity, the sun; middle age, Mars; advanced age, Jupiter; and decrepitude and dissolution, Saturn.

HOW THE ELEMENTS ARE IN THE HEAVENS, IN STARS, IN DEVILS, IN ANGELS, AND LASTLY IN GOD HIMSELF

By Eliphas Levi

It is the unanimous consent of all Platonists, that as in the original and exemplary World, all things are in all; so also in this corporeal world, all things are in all; so also the Elements are not only in these inferior bodies, but also in the Heavens, in Stars in Devils, in Angels, and lastly in God, the maker and original example of all things. Now in these inferior bodies the Elements are accompanied with much gross matter; but in the Heavens the Elements are with their natures and virtues, viz., after a celestial and more excellent manner than in sublunary things. For the firmness of the Celestial Earth is there without the grossness of water; and the agility of the Air without running over its bounds; the heat of Fire without burning, only shining and giving life to all things by its heat. Amongst the Stars, also, some are fiery, as Mars and Sol; airy, as Jupiter and Venus; watery, as Saturn and Mercury; and earthy, such as inhabit the eighth *Orb* and the Moon (which, notwithstanding, by many is accounted watery), seeing, as if it were Earth, it attracts to itself the celestial waters, with which, being imbibed, it doth, by reason of its nearness to us, pour out and communicate to us. There are, also, amongst the Signs, some fiery, some earthy, some airy, some watery; the Elements rule them also in the Heavens, distributing to them these four threefold considerations of every Element, viz., the beginning, middle and end: So Aires possesseth the beginning of fire, Leo the progress and increase, and Sagittarius the end. Taurus the beginning of the earth, Virgo the progress, Capricorn the end. Gemini the beginning of the air, Libra the progress, Aquarius the end. Cancer the beginning of water, Scorpius the middle, and Pisces the end. Of the mixtions, therefore, of these

Planets and Signs, together with the Elements, are all bodies made. Moreover, Devils also are upon this account distinguished the one from the other, so that some are called fiery, some earthy, some airy, and some watery. Hence, also, those four Infernal Rivers—fiery Phlegethon, airy Cocytus, watery Styx, earthy Acheron. Also in the Gospel we read of hell fire, and eternal fire, into which the cursed shall be commanded to go; and in the Revelation we read of a lake of fire, and Isaiah speaks of the damned that the Lord will smite them with corrupt air. And in Job, they shall skip from the waters of the snow to extremity of heat; and in the same we read, that the Earth is dark, and covered with the darkness of death and miserable darkness. Moreover, also, these Elements are placed in the Angels in Heaven and the blessed Intelligences. There is in them a stability of their essence, which is an earthly virtue, in which is the steadfast seat of God; also their mercy and piety is a watery cleansing virtue. Hence by the Psalmist they are called Waters, where he, speaking of the Heavens, saith, Who rulest the Waters that are higher than the Heavens. Also in them their subtile breath is Air, and their love is shining Fire. Hence they are called in Scripture the Wings of the Wind; and in another place the Psalmist speaks of them, Who makest Angels thy Spirits and thy Ministers a flaming fire. Also according to orders of Angels, some are fiery, as Seraphim, and Authorities and Powers; earthy, as Cherubim; watery, as Thrones and Archangels; airy, as Dominions and Principalities. Do we not also read of the original maker of all things, that the earth shall be opened and bring forth a Savior? It is not spoken of the same that he shall be a fountain of living Water, cleansing and regenerating? Is not the same Spirit breathing the breath of life; and the same, according to Moses' and Paul's testimony, a consuming Fire? That Elements, therefore, are to be found everywhere, and in all things after their manner, no man can deny: First in these inferior bodies seculent and gross, and in celestials more pure and clear; but in supercelestials living, and in all respects blessed. Elements, therefore, in the exemplary world are *Ideas* of things to be produced, in Intelligences are distributed powers, in Heavens are virtues, and in inferior bodies gross forms.

www.ingramcontent.com/pod-product-compliance
Lightning Source LLC
LaVergne TN
LVHW041504070426
835507LV00009B/800